Managing Discovery of Electronic Information: A Pocket Guide for Judges

Barbara J. Rothstein, Ronald J. Hedges, and Elizabeth C. Wiggins

Federal Judicial Center
2007

This Federal Judicial Center publication was undertaken in furtherance of the Center's statutory mission to develop and conduct education programs for judicial branch employees. The views expressed are those of the authors and not necessarily those of the Federal Judicial Center.

Blank page for correct double-sided printing.

Contents

Blank page for correct double-sided printing.

Preface

This pocket guide is designed to help federal judges manage the discovery of electronically stored information (ESI). It encourages judges to actively manage those cases involving ESI, raising points for consideration by the parties rather than awaiting the parties' identification and argument of the matters. The guide covers issues unique to the discovery of ESI, including its scope, the allocation of costs, the form of production, the waiver of privilege and work-product protection, and the preservation of data and spoliation. As you are reading, you may encounter some unfamiliar terms. Many of these terms are defined in a glossary at the end of the guide. A note of appreciation goes to Judge Lee H. Rosenthal (S.D. Tex.), Ken Withers (the Sedona Conference), and John Rabiej (Administrative Office of the U.S. Courts) for their suggestions, which improved this publication. I hope you find the guide useful in meeting the challenges presented by the discovery of ESI.

Barbara Jacobs Rothstein
Director, Federal Judicial Center

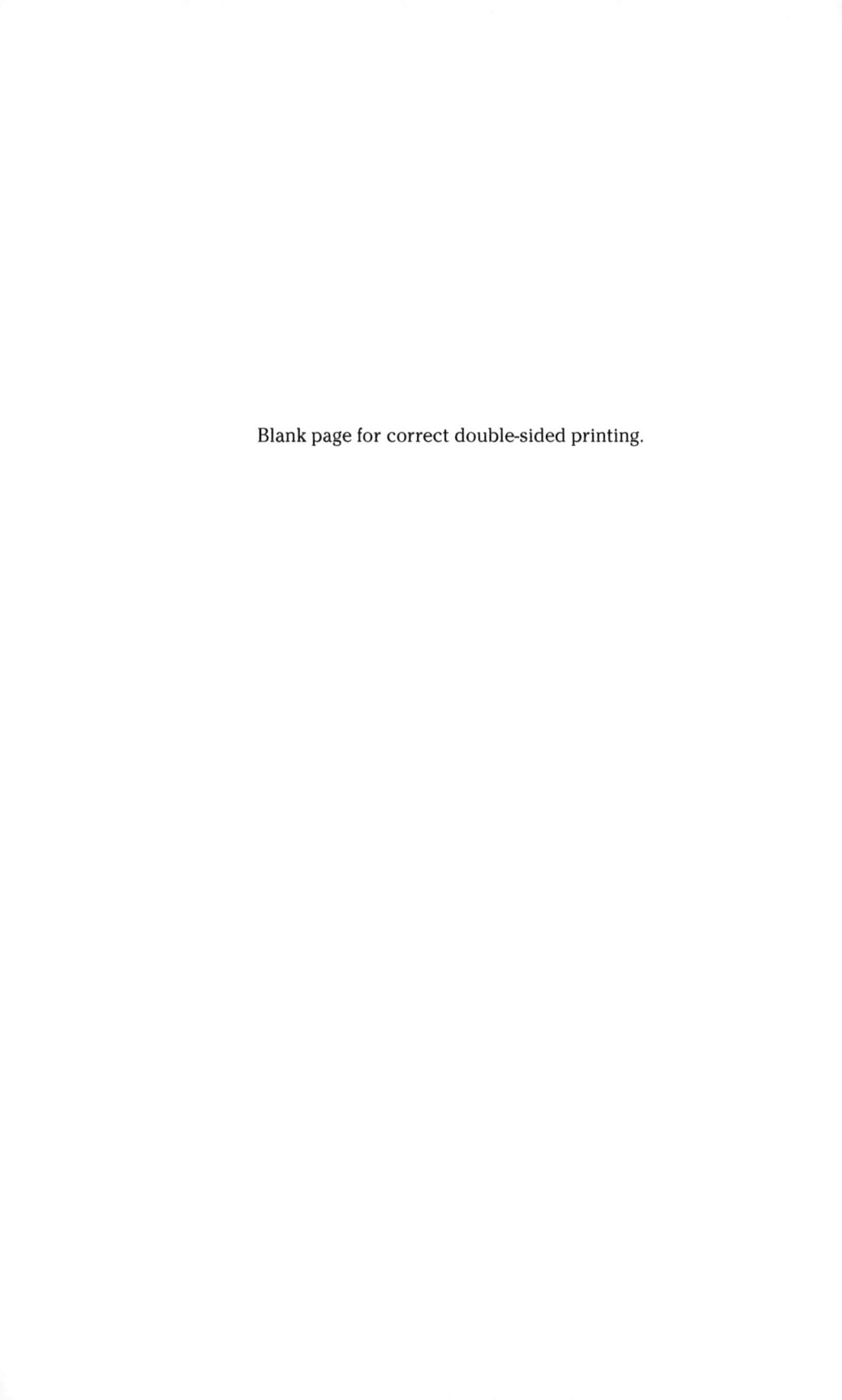
Blank page for correct double-sided printing.

Introduction

It is a fact of modern life that an enormous volume of information is created, exchanged, and stored electronically. Conventional documents originate as computer files, e-mail is taking the place of both telephone calls and postal letters, and many, if not most, commercial activities are transacted using computer-based business processes. Electronically stored information (ESI) is commonplace in our personal lives and in the operation of businesses, public entities, and private organizations.

In the past decade, discovery involving word-processed documents, spreadsheets, e-mail, and other electronically stored information has become more routine: Once seen only in large cases involving sophisticated entities, it is now seen in routine civil cases and in many criminal cases. In some cases, ESI does not raise any issue, or it is converted to paper and is exchanged in the traditional manner. In other cases, disputes arise as to the scope of discovery, the form in which ESI is produced, whether inadvertent production of ESI will lead to waiver of attorney–client privilege or work-product protection, the shifting of costs from producing to requesting parties, and the preservation of ESI and related spoliation allegations. For example, in some cases a dispute may surface when one party finds that digital files have been delivered in a format that is not readily usable. In other cases, technology issues may remain submerged until later in the pretrial process when one side accuses the other of spoliation because routine digital file management practices remained in place after the complaint was filed, resulting in the deletion of computer files.

The court may minimize such disputes by encouraging lawyers and parties to identify, in the earliest stages of litigation, potential problems in the discovery of ESI and possible resolutions to those problems, and by intervening before misunderstandings and disputes lead to significant delay and costs. Case law addressing conventional discovery and ESI-related discovery, the Federal Rules of Civil Procedure, local rules,[1] the *Manual for Complex Litigation*,

---

1. *See, e.g.*, U.S. Dist. Ct. Rules E.D. & W.D. Ark., L. R. 26.1; U.S. Dist. Ct. Rules D.N.J., L. Civ. R. 26.1; U.S. Dist. Ct. Rules M.D. Pa., L. Civ. R. 26.1; and U.S. Dist. Ct. Rules D. Wyo., L. Civ. R. 26.1, App. D. *See also* Ad Hoc Committee for Electronic Discovery of the United States District Court for the District of Delaware, *Default Standard for Discovery of Electronic Documents* (http://www.ded.uscourts. gov/OrdersMain.htm); U.S. District Court for the District of Kansas, *Guidelines for*

Fourth, and various legal publications offer management tools for the judge's use.[2] Amendments to the Federal Rules of Civil Procedure that specifically address the discovery of ESI went into effect December 1, 2006.[3]

Discovery involving ESI may require more intensive judicial involvement than required by conventional discovery. The purpose of this guide is to identify problems that recur during the course of electronic discovery and to present management tools for responding to them.

What Is Electronically Stored Information and How Does It Differ from Conventional Information?

Among others things, ESI includes e-mails, webpages, word processing files, and databases stored in the memory of computers, magnetic disks (such as computer hard drives and floppy disks), optical disks (such as DVDs and CDs), and flash memory (such as "thumb" or "flash" drives). Federal Rules of Civil Procedure 26 and 34, which went into effect December 1, 2006, use the term "electronically stored information" rather than the term "data compilation" and identify it as a distinctive category of information subject to discovery obligations on par with "documents" and "things."

ESI differs from conventional, paper information in several ways. The volume of ESI is almost always exponentially greater than paper information, and it may be located in multiple places. For example, draft and final versions of a single paper memorandum may be stored electronically in multiple places (e.g., on the computer hard drives of the document's creator, reviewers, and recipients; on the company server; on laptops and home computers;

the *Discovery of Electronically Stored Information* (http://www.ksd.uscourts.gov/guidelines/electronicdiscoveryguidelines.pdf).

2. *See also* American Bar Association, Civil Discovery Standards 57–76 (2004) (Standards 29–33) (at http://www.abanet.org/litigation/discoverystandards/); The Sedona Principles: Best Practices, Recommendations & Principles for Addressing Electronic Document Discovery (Sedona Conference Working Group Series Jan. 2004) [hereinafter *The Sedona Principles*] (updated version available at http://www.thesedonaconference.org/content/miscFiles/publications_html).

3. These rules can be found at http://www.uscourts.gov/rules/index.html.

and on backup tapes). Market research tells us that the average employee sends or receives about 50 messages per working day,[4] which translates into more than 1,200,000 messages a year for an organization of 100 employees.

Also, although the possibility that paper documents may be damaged, altered, or destroyed has always been a concern, the dynamic, mutable nature of ESI presents new challenges. For example, computer systems automatically recycle and reuse memory space, altering potentially relevant information without any specific direction or even knowledge of the operator. Merely opening a digital file changes information about that file.

Some aspects of ESI have no counterpart in print media, metadata being the most obvious. Metadata, which most computer users never see, provide information about an electronic file, such as the date it was created, its author, when and by whom it was edited, what edits were made, and, in the case of e-mail, the history of its transmission. Also, some computer-based transactions do not result in a conventional document, but instead are represented in integrated databases. Even less-complex ESI may be incomprehensible and unusable when separated from the system that created it. For example, a spreadsheet produced in portable document format (PDF) may be useless because embedded information, such as computational formulas, cannot be seen or discerned. Finally, deleting an electronic document does not get rid of it, as shredding a paper document would. An electronic document may be recovered from the hard drive, to the extent it has not been overwritten, and may be available on the computers of other people and on archival media or backup tapes used for disaster recovery rather than archival purposes.

> **How ESI differs from paper information:**
>
> Volume
> Variety of sources
> Dynamic quality
> Hidden information: metadata and embedded data
> Dependent on system that created it
> Deleting doesn't delete it

These differences between ESI and conventional information have important implications for discovery. For example, the dynamic nature of ESI makes it vital that a data producer institute "lit-

---

4. Microsoft, *Survey Finds Workers Average Only Three Productive Days Per Week* (Mar. 15, 2005) <http://www.microsoft.com/presspass/press/2005/mar05/03-15ThreeProductiveDaysPr.mspx> (visited Jan. 3, 2007) (U.S. workers reported they receive an average of 56 e-mail messages per day).

igation holds" to preserve information that may be discoverable, often even before the lawsuit is filed. Moreover, the volume and multiple sources of ESI may lead to disputes about the scope of discovery and may make review to identify and segregate privileged information more difficult, increasing the likelihood of its inadvertent production even when the producing party has taken steps to avoid it. In addition, because deleted or backup information may be available, parties may request its production, even though restoring, retrieving, and producing it may require expensive and burdensome computer forensic work that is out of proportion to the reasonable discovery needs of the requesting party.

Early Consideration of ESI—Rules 26(f) and 16

Exchanging information in electronic form has significant benefits—it can substantially reduce copying, transport, and storage costs; enable the requesting party to more easily review, organize, and manage information; facilitate the use of computerized litigation support systems; and set the stage for the use of digital evidence presentation systems during pretrial and trial proceedings. To ensure that these benefits are achieved and any problems associated with ESI are minimized, attorneys and parties should address ESI in the earliest stages of litigation, and judges should encourage them to do so.

All too often, attorneys view their obligation to "meet and confer" under Federal Rule of Civil Procedure 26(f) as a perfunctory exercise. When ESI is involved, judges should insist that a meaningful Rule 26(f) conference take place and that a meaningful discovery plan be submitted. Amended Rule 26(f) directs parties to discuss any issues relating to disclosure or discovery of ESI, including the form or forms in which it should be produced. More specifically, the parties should inquire into whether there will be discovery of ESI at all; what information each party has in electronic form and where that information resides; whether the information to be discovered has been deleted or is available only on backup tapes or legacy systems; the anticipated schedule for production and the format and media of that production; the difficulty and cost of producing the information and reallocation of costs, if appropriate; and the responsibilities of each party to preserve ESI.[5]

Amended Rule 26(f) also directs parties to discuss issues related to claims of privilege or protection as trial-preparation material. If the parties agree on a procedure to assert such claims after production, they should discuss whether to ask the court to include their agreement in an order. (See related discussion, *infra* page 14.)

For the "meet and confer" process to be effective, attorneys must be familiar with how their clients use computers on a daily basis and understand what information is available, how routine computer operations may change it, and what is entailed in producing it. Attorneys need to identify those persons who are most knowledgeable about the client's computer system and meet with them well in advance of the Rule 26 conference; it may also be advisable to have those persons present at the conference.

> **Discussion topics for a Rule 26(f) conference:**
>
> What ESI is available and where it resides
>
> Ease/difficulty and cost of producing information
>
> Schedule and format of production
>
> Preservation of information
>
> Agreements about privilege or work-product protection

The Rule 16 conference and order afford the court the opportunity, early in the case, to discuss and memorialize the agreements or shared understandings that parties reach in their "meet and confer" session, and to resolve disputes that may have arisen. Amended Rule 16(b) provides that scheduling orders may include provisions for disclosure or discovery of ESI and any agreements the parties reach for asserting claims of privilege or of protection as trial-preparation material after production.

ESI and Rule 26(a)(1) Disclosures

Rule 26(a)(1) requires disclosure of the identities of individuals likely to have discoverable information, as well as "a copy of, or a description by category and location of, all documents, data compilations, and tangible things" that the disclosing party may use

---

5. Specific topics for discussion related to the preservation of information are listed in the *Manual for Complex Litigation, Fourth* § 40.25(2) (Federal Judicial Center 2004) [hereinafter *MCL 4th*].

to support its claims or defenses, unless solely for impeachment. Effective December 1, 2006, the term "data compilations" was changed to "electronically stored information," clarifying a party's duty to include ESI in its disclosures. Automatic disclosures must be made "at or within 14 days after the Rule 26(f) conference unless a different time is set by stipulation or court order."

The *Manual for Complex Litigation, Fourth* emphasizes that the parties have a duty to conduct a reasonable investigation pursuant to disclosure, particularly when a party possesses extensive computerized data, which may be subject to disclosure or later identification.[6] This task may be daunting for a party with voluminous ESI to identify, especially if that information is not readily accessible. With respect to less-accessible ESI, *Moore's Federal Practice* suggests that the following disclosures and investigation should satisfy the basic requirements of Rule 26(a)(1):

> The disclosing party should identify the nature of its computer system—including back-up system, network system, and e-mail system—as well as any software applications used to operate those systems. However, the disclosing party should not be required to attempt to search back-up systems or to retrieve deleted files in an exhaustive effort to locate all potentially relevant evidence as part of this initial disclosure obligation. Further, a party should not be held liable for sanctions or other penalties for failing to disclose this evidence as part of its initial disclosure obligation, even when that evidence is subsequently used in the litigation. The difficulty in retrieving this information provides "substantial justification" to excuse such an exhaustive search effort.[7]

ESI and Scope of Discovery Under Rules 26(b)(1) and 26(b)(2)

The central issue in almost all discovery management is the determination of scope. Under Rule 26(b)(1), parties may obtain discovery relevant to the "claim or defense of any party" that is not privi-

---

6. *MCL 4th, supra* note 5, § 11.13.
7. J.M. Moore, Moore's Federal Practice § 37A.21[1] (3d ed. 2005) (footnote omitted).

leged or protected as trial preparation material. In addition, the court may order discovery of information relevant to the "subject matter involved in the action" for "good cause." Under either standard, the principles of proportionality set out in Rule 26(b)(2)(C) apply.[8] Rule 26(b)(2)(C) provides:

> The frequency or extent of use of the discovery methods otherwise permitted under these rules and by any local rule shall be limited by the court if it determines that: (i) the discovery sought is unreasonably cumulative or duplicative, or is obtainable from some other source that is more convenient, less burdensome, or less expensive; (ii) the party seeking discovery has had ample opportunity by discovery in the action to obtain the information sought; or (iii) the burden or expense of the proposed discovery outweighs its likely benefit, taking into account the needs of the case, the amount in controversy, the parties' resources, the importance of the issues at stake in the litigation, and the importance of the proposed discovery in resolving the issues. The court may act upon its own initiative after reasonable notice or pursuant to a motion under Rule 26(c).

In the context of ESI, whether the proportionality analysis of Rule 26(b)(2)(C) is satisfied often turns on the type of computer data being sought. Assuming the requested information is relevant to the claims or defenses or the subject matter of the dispute and is not subject to a claim of privilege or protection, the production of active data, available to the responding party in the ordinary course of business, is most likely to satisfy the proportionality test. Active electronic records are generally those currently being created, received, or processed, or that need to be accessed frequently and quickly. Systems data, which include such things as when people logged on and off a computer or network, the applications and passwords they used, and what websites they visited, may be more remote and more costly to produce. Other types of data are even more removed from what is available in the ordinary course of business and may involve substantial costs and time and active intervention of computer specialists. These types of data include offline archival media, backup tapes designed for restoring computer systems in the event of disaster, deleted files, and legacy

---

8. Prior to December 1, 2006, Rule 26(b)(2)(C) was Rule 26(b)(2).

data, which were created on now-obsolete computer systems with obsolete operating and computer software.[9] Even active data may involve substantial burdens to produce—for example, when vast amounts are requested or when data are requested in a form that requires the reprogramming of databases. When hard-to-access information is of potential interest, the court should encourage lawyers to negotiate a two-tiered approach in which they first sort through the information that can be provided from easily accessed sources and then determine whether it is necessary to search the less-accessible sources.

Rule 26(b)(2)(B) and the accompanying Committee Note embrace this two-tiered approach. The rule establishes the following procedure for the discovery of not reasonably accessible ESI:

> (B) A party need not provide discovery of electronically stored information from sources that the party identifies as not reasonably accessible because of undue burden or cost. On motion to compel discovery or for a protective order, the party from whom discovery is sought must show that the information is not reasonably accessible because of undue burden or cost. If that showing is made, the court may nonetheless order discovery from such sources if the requesting party shows good cause, considering the limitations of Rule 26(b)(2)(C). The court may specify conditions for the discovery.

The requesting party may need discovery to test the assertion that the information is not reasonably accessible. Such discovery may involve taking depositions of those knowledgeable about the responding party's information systems; some form of inspection of the data sources; and requiring the responding party to conduct a sampling of information contained on the sources identified as not reasonably accessible. Sampling of the less-accessible source can help refine the search parameters and determine the benefits and burdens associated with a fuller search.[10]

---

9. *See also* Zubulake v. UBS Warburg LLC, 217 F.R.D. 309, 318–19 (S.D.N.Y. 2003) (describing the media on which ESI is maintained, and distinguishing online, active data, nearline data, offline storage/archives, and backup tapes).

10. *See* McPeek v. Ashcroft, 202 F.R.D. 31 (D.D.C. 2001); McPeek v. Ashcroft, 212 F.R.D. 33 (D.D.C. 2003); Hagemeyer N. Am., Inc. v. Gateway Data Sciences Corp., 222 F.R.D. 594 (E.D. Wis. 2004) (all supporting the use of sampling to tailor the scope of further discovery).

Even if it is determined that a source of ESI is not reasonably accessible, the requesting party may obtain discovery by showing good cause subject to the limitations of Rule 26(b)(2)(C). The Committee Note suggests that, in determining whether to allow the discovery, the judge consider the following:

> (1) the specificity of the discovery request; (2) the quantity of information available from other and more easily accessed sources; (3) the failure to produce relevant information that seems likely to have existed but is no longer available on more easily accessed sources; (4) the likelihood of finding relevant, responsive information that cannot be obtained from other, more easily accessed sources; (5) predictions as to the importance and usefulness of the further information; (6) the importance of the issues at stake in the litigation; and (7) the parties' resources.

In making this determination, the court has a variety of available tools, including

- ordering the parties to examine the information that is available from reasonably accessible sources before requiring discovery into sources that are identified as not reasonably accessible;
- ensuring that the requesting party makes a specific and tailored discovery request;
- ordering sampling of the sources identified as not reasonably accessible to assess the costs and burdens of production and the likelihood of finding responsive information and its usefulness to the litigation;
- ordering limited discovery into the costs and burdens of accessing the information from the sources identified as not reasonably accessible and into the basis for believing that they do, or do not, contain information likely to be important to the case and not available from other, accessible sources, such as depositions of the responding party's computer system personnel; and
- ordering the requesting party to pay all or part of the reasonable costs of producing the information from sources identified as not reasonably accessible. (See the discussion in the next section.)

Allocation of Costs

In cases involving vast amounts of ESI, or ESI that is not available from reasonably accessible sources, the cost to the producing party in locating the information, reviewing it for privilege, and otherwise preparing it for production may be much greater than in conventional discovery. At the same time, the cost of copying and transporting the information is practically eliminated and the cost to the requesting party of searching the information may be reduced because it can be done electronically.

In such cases, it may be appropriate to shift at least some of the production costs from the producing party to the requesting party. Two major cases—*Rowe Entertainment, Inc. v. William Morris Agency, Inc.*[11] and *Zubulake v. UBS Warburg LLC*[12]—have introduced multifactor tests to determine when cost shifting is appropriate.

In *Rowe*, a racial discrimination case, the defendants objected to the production of e-mail information from backup media on the grounds that such discovery was unlikely to provide relevant information and would invade the privacy of nonparties, and they requested that the plaintiffs bear the costs if production was nevertheless required. The court concluded that the e-mail information sought by the plaintiffs was relevant and that a blanket order precluding its discovery was unjustified. However, balancing eight factors derived from case law, the court required the plaintiffs to pay for the recovery and production of the e-mail backups, except for the cost of screening for relevance and privilege. The eight *Rowe* factors were (1) the specificity of the discovery requests; (2) the likelihood of discovering critical information; (3) the availability of such information from other sources; (4) the purposes for which the responding party maintains the requested data; (5) the relative benefit to the parties of obtaining the information; (6) the total cost associated with production; (7) the relative ability of each party to control costs and its incentive to do so; and (8) the resources available to each party.[13]

Zubulake, a gender discrimination case, also involved the production of e-mails that existed only on backup tapes and other archived media. After concluding that the plaintiff's request was rel-

---

11. 205 F.R.D. 421 (S.D.N.Y.), *aff'd*, 53 Fed. R. Serv. 3d 296 (S.D.N.Y. 2002).
12. 217 F.R.D. 309 (S.D.N.Y. 2003).
13. *Rowe*, 205 F.R.D. at 428–29.

evant to her claims, the court held that the usual rules of discovery generally apply when the data are in accessible format, but that cost shifting could be considered when data were relatively inaccessible, such as on backup tapes, and substituted seven factors for the *Rowe* factors. The *Zubulake* factors, in order of importance, were (1) the extent to which the request is specifically tailored to discover relevant information; (2) the availability of such information from other sources; (3) the total cost of production, compared to the amount in controversy; (4) the total cost of production, compared to the resources available to each party; (5) the relative ability of each party to control costs and its incentive to do so; (6) the importance of the issues at stake in the litigation; and (7) the relative benefits to the parties of obtaining the information. The court emphasized that the factors should not be applied mechanistically and should be weighted according to their importance.

Other courts have adopted or modified the *Rowe* and *Zubulake* formulations.[14] Moreover, the Committee Note to Rule 26(b)(2)(B) makes explicit the authority to shift costs when information that is not reasonably accessible is being produced.

Zubulake also set forth a sensible approach for assessing costs when a large number of backup tapes are involved. Following the order in the above case, the defendants restored and reviewed 5 of the 77 backup tapes of interest; they found approximately 600 messages deemed to be responsive at a cost of about $19,000. Based on this work, the defendants were able to estimate the cost of restoring and reviewing the entire 77-tape collection. Considering the seven factors, the court determined that the balance tipped

---

14. *See* Wiginton v. CB Richard Ellis, Inc., 2004 U.S. Dist. LEXIS 15722, *13 (N.D. Ill. Aug. 10, 2004) (adds the importance of the requested discovery in resolving the issues of the litigation to the *Zubulake* factors); Multitechnology Servs., L.P. v. Verizon Southwest, 2004 WL 1553480 (N.D. Tex. July 12, 2004) (analyzes application to shift costs for "relevant and discoverable" electronic information under Rule 26(c) and apparently rejects *Zubulake*'s applicability and concludes that "requiring the parties to evenly shoulder the expense is the most effective resolution because it balances the benefit of the discovery . . . and provides . . . [an] incentive to manage costs it incurs"; also held that "it is appropriate to classify the expense as court costs that can be recovered by the prevailing party"); Hagemeyer N. Am., Inc. v. Gateway Data Sciences Corp., 222 F.R.D. 594, 599–603 (E.D. Wis. 2004) (analyzes cost-shifting tests and concludes that "*Zubulake* brought the cost-shifting analysis closest to the Rule 26(b)(2) proportionality test" and adopts it).

slightly against cost shifting and required the defendants to bear 75% of the restoration costs.[15]

Discovery from Nonparties

Discovery from nonparties is likely to be more frequent when the parties are seeking ESI than when they are seeking conventional paper documents. Many businesses and individuals depend on telecommunications companies, Internet service providers, and computer network owners for computer services, and these non-parties may be the source for relevant and discoverable ESI, especially e-mail messages. Even larger companies routinely outsource their computer-management and data-storage functions to contractors and consultants. Rule 45, effective December 1, 2006, conforms the provisions for subpoenas to other changes in the rules related to the discovery of ESI. Parallel to amended Rule 26(b)(2), Rule 45 introduces the concept of sources that are not reasonably accessible. It also addresses the form for the production of ESI, adds a procedure for asserting claims of privilege or of protection as trial-preparation materials, and allows for the testing or sampling of ESI. Although Rule 45 has no equivalent to the Rule 26(f) "meet and confer" process, parties seeking discovery under Rule 45 should be encouraged to meet informally with respondents and discuss the scope of the subpoena, the desired form of response, protection for privileged and protected information, and the allocation of discovery costs.

---

15. This case is commonly referred to as *Zubulake III*, 216 F.R.D. 280 (S.D.N.Y 2003). *Zubulake II*, 230 F.R.D. 290 (S.D.N.Y. 2003), addressed the plaintiff's request to release a sealed transcript. *Zubulake IV*, 220 F.R.D. 212 (S.D.N.Y. 2003), addressed the plaintiff's request for sanctions (including an adverse inference instruction) arising out of the failure to preserve backup tapes and deletion of isolated e-mails. In ruling on the request, the court considered the obligation of a party to preserve digital information. In *Zubulake V*, 229 F.R.D. 422 (S.D.N.Y. 2004), the court imposed sanctions for deleting relevant e-mail. In *Zubulake VI*, 231 F.R.D. 159 (S.D.N.Y. 2005), the court denied a defense motion (brought by new counsel) to assert an affirmative defense. In *Zubulake VII*, 382 F. Supp. 2d 536 (S.D.N.Y. 2005), the court addressed in limine motions. On April 6, 2005, a jury awarded the plaintiff $9.1 million in compensatory damages and $20.1 million in punitive damages.

Form of Production

Electronically stored information can be produced in a variety of forms or formats, each with distinctive advantages and disadvantages. The form may have important implications for how easily, if at all, the information can be electronically searched, whether relevant information is obscured or sensitive information is revealed, and how the information can be used in later stages of the litigation. For example, ESI may be produced as a TIFF or PDF file, which is essentially a photograph of an electronic document. Alternatively, ESI may be produced in "native format," that is, the form in which the information was created and is used in the normal course of operations. Part Two of *Effective Use of Courtroom Technology*[16] reviews in depth the various digital formats in which documents, photographs, videos, and other materials can be produced and the related issues of cost and usability.[17] Recent decisions, including *Hagenbuch v. Sistemi Elettronici Industriali S.R.L.*[18] and *Williams v. Sprint/United Management Co.*,[19] have addressed the form of production.

Rule 34 was amended to provide a procedure for addressing the form of ESI because this issue simply did not arise with respect to paper discovery. The rule permits the requesting party to designate the form or forms in which it wants ESI produced, and it requires the responding party to identify the form in which it intends to produce the information if the requesting party does not specify a form or if the responding party objects to a form that the requesting party specifies. It also requires the parties to meet and confer if there is a dispute about form of production and provides that in the absence of a party agreement or court order, the responding party must produce electronically stored information either in a form or

---

16. Effective Use of Courtroom Technology: A Judge's Guide to Pretrial and Trial (Federal Judicial Center 2001).

17. Also see the term *file format* in the glossary.

18. 2006 WL 665005 (N.D. Ill. Mar. 8, 2006) (holding that production of ESI as TIFF images was insufficient and ordering production of ESI in its original format).

19. 230 F.R.D. 640 (D. Kan. 2005) (holding that the production of spreadsheets in static format was insufficient because the mathematical formulas, text exceeding cell size, and metadata were eliminated, and that the defendant should have preserved and produced the spreadsheets in native format or taken other measures to preserve and produce the nonapparent information).

forms in which it is ordinarily maintained or in a form or forms that are reasonably usable.

In resolving disputes over the form of production, considerations for the court include the following:

- What alternatives are available? What are their benefits and drawbacks for the requesting and responding parties?

- If the responding party is not producing information in the form in which it is ordinarily maintained, is the party producing it in a form that is reasonably usable to the requesting party?

- If the requesting party disputes that the proposed form of production is reasonably usable, what limits its use? Has the responding party stripped features, such as searchability, or metadata or embedded data that may be important? If so, what is the justification?

Waiver of Privilege or Work-Product Protection

The volume of ESI searched and produced in response to a discovery request can be enormous, and characteristics of certain types of ESI (e.g., embedded data, metadata, threads of e-mail communications and e-mail attachments) make it difficult to review for privilege and work-product protection. Thus, the inadvertent disclosure of privileged or protected material during production is a substantial risk that persists even if expensive and time-consuming steps are taken to identify and segregate it. To facilitate discovery, parties have entered into agreements that help minimize the risk of waiver. Under what is commonly called a "quick peek" agreement, the responding party provides requested material without a thorough review for privilege or protection, but with the explicit understanding that its production does not waive any privilege or protection. The requesting party then designates via Rule 34 the specific documents it would like produced. The responding party then has the opportunity to review the documents that have been specifically requested and withhold those that are privileged or protected. Alternatively, under "claw back" agreements, the parties typically review the material for privilege or protection before it is produced but agree to a procedure for the return of privileged or protected information that is inadvertently produced within a reasonable time of its discovery.

Amended Rule 26(f) encourages parties to discuss whether they can agree on these or similar arrangements, recognizing the increased likelihood of inadvertent production of privileged or protected information and the commensurately increased cost and delay required for effective preproduction review.[20] Amended Rule 16(b) provides that if the parties are able to agree, the court may include their agreement in the case-management order. The rule, however, does not authorize the court to require the parties to enter into such an arrangement, absent their agreement. Because substantive privilege (and waiver) rules are beyond the scope of the Federal Rules of Civil Procedure, the rules recognize that although such an agreement is binding among the parties, it may or may not bind third parties.[21] Including the parties' agreements in a court order clarifies the effect of inadvertent production on the waiver of privilege or protection between the parties and bolsters the argument that no waiver has occurred as to third parties in other litigation.

In addition, amended Rule 26(b)(5) establishes procedures for asserting privilege or work-product protection claims after production. Under these procedures, the party claiming that already-produced information is subject to a claim of privilege or protection may notify any party that received the information of the claim and the basis for it. The receiving party must then promptly return,

---

20. Some early decisions have refused to enforce such agreements (*MCL 4th*, *supra* note 5, § 11.431). Other opinions and commentary have raised concerns or limitations about the use of such agreements. *See* R.J. Hedges, "A Critical Appraisal of Proposed Amendment to Federal Rule of Civil Procedure 26(b)(5)(B)," vol. 5, no. 2, Digital Discovery & e-Evidence 4 (Mar. 2005) (will production of privileged materials under an agreement be deemed a waiver vis-à-vis a third party?); Maldonado v. New Jersey, 225 F.R.D. 120, 141 (D.N.J. 2004) (such agreements may lead to the disqualification of attorneys if, even after a privileged document is returned, the attorneys' temporary possession of the document "creates a substantial taint on any future proceedings"). Also see *The Sedona Principles*, *supra* note 2, Comment 10.d, regarding concerns raised by claw back or quick peek agreements.

21. *See* Hopson v. Mayor and City Council of Baltimore, 232 F.R.D. 228 (D. Md. 2005) (reviewing the conflicting case law about whether an inadvertent disclosure of privileged or protected information constitutes a waiver and whether a confidentiality order binds third parties in parallel or future litigation, and describing the benefits of embodying any waiver agreement in a court order).

sequester, or destroy the information and any copies it has and may not use or disclose the information until the claim is resolved; if the party has disclosed the information before being notified, it must take reasonable steps to retrieve it. The receiving party may promptly present the information to the court under seal for a determination of the claim.

The accompanying Committee Note to Rule 26(b)(5) emphatically states that these procedures do not address the substantive questions of whether privilege or work-product protection has been waived or forfeited; courts should rely on developed principles to determine whether, and under what circumstances, waiver results from inadvertent production.[22] For example, unreasonable delay in seeking the return of privileged information may give rise to a waiver. The note also emphasizes that agreed-on procedures under Rules 26(f) and 16(b) would take precedence over the rule-based ones.

Any assertion of privilege raises the question of how that assertion is to be tested. The accepted practice is, of course, in camera inspection of the material by the court. In cases involving ESI, however, the judge may have to grapple with whether the sheer volume of information requires new methods of review, such as sampling or, in the most difficult cases, the use of a special master.

Preservation of ESI

As noted above, amended Rule 26(f) and the accompanying Committee Note direct parties to discuss issues regarding the preserva-

---

22. A proposed new Federal Rule of Evidence 502 was published for comment in August 2006. It (1) provides that inadvertent disclosure of privileged or protected information in connection with a federal proceeding constitutes a waiver only if the party did not take reasonable precautions to prevent disclosure and did not make reasonable and prompt efforts to rectify the error; (2) provides that when a confidentiality order governing disclosure is entered in a federal proceeding, according to terms agreed to by the parties, the order's terms are enforceable against nonparties in any other federal or state proceedings; and (3) codifies the proposition that parties can enter an agreement to limit the effect of waiver by disclosure between or among themselves, and makes clear that if the parties want protection from a finding of waiver by disclosure in separate litigation, the agreement must be made part of a court order. The proposed rule also limits the circumstances in which a subject-matter waiver should be found and includes a provision on selective waiver.

tion of discoverable information, particularly with respect to ESI because of its dynamic, mutable nature. In doing so, parties should attempt to balance the need to preserve relevant information and the need to continue routine computer operations critical to a party's activities.

The court may help ensure that parties meet their responsibilities for preserving information and avoid allegations of spoliation by reviewing with them steps for establishing and implementing an effective data-preservation policy. These include (1) allowing the party's "discovery liaison" to readily describe information systems, storage, and retention policies to the opposing party and the court; (2) interviewing key employees to determine sources of information; (3) affirmatively and repeatedly communicating litigation holds to all affected parties and monitoring compliance on an ongoing basis; (4) integrating discovery responsibilities with routine retention policies; (5) actively managing and monitoring document collections; (6) thoroughly documenting and demonstrating the efficacy of the preservation process; and (7) preparing to take responsibility for ensuring that information is preserved, collected, and produced.[23]

In some cases, a preservation order that clearly defines the obligations of the producing party may minimize the risk that relevant evidence will be deliberately or inadvertently destroyed, may help ensure information is retrieved when it is most accessible (i.e., before it has been deleted or removed from active online data), and may protect the producing party from sanctions.[24]

The *Manual for Complex Litigation, Fourth* provides guidance about what type of preservation order is most useful, and under what circumstances an order should be entered.[25] Because a blanket preservation order may unduly interfere in a party's day-to-day operations, may be prohibitively expensive, and may actually compound the information to be searched and produced, any order should be narrowly drawn to preserve relevant matter without imposing undue burdens.[26] Early in the case, the court should

---

23. This list is based on the discussion in *Zubulake V*, 229 F.R.D. 422 (S.D.N.Y. 2004).

24. Treppel v. Biovail Corp., 2006 WL 278170, *5 (S.D.N.Y. Feb. 6, 2006) (describing the benefits of preservation orders).

25. *MCL 4th, supra* note 5, § 11.442.

26. For an example of a broad data-preservation order, see *Pueblo of Laguna v. United States*, 60 Fed. Cl. 133, 141–43 (Ct. Cl. 2004).

discuss with the parties whether an order is needed and, if so, the scope, duration, method of data preservation, and other terms that will preserve relevant matter without imposing undue burdens.[27] In crafting the order, it is important to know from the responding party what data-management systems are routinely used, the volume of data affected, and the costs and technical feasibility of implementing the order. Preservation orders should ordinarily include provisions permitting the destruction of information under specified circumstances. Preservation orders may, for example, exclude from preservation specified categories of documents or data whose cost of preservation substantially outweighs their relevance in the litigation, particularly if the information can be obtained from other sources. Moreover, as issues in the case are narrowed, the court should reduce the scope of the order.

A closing note about preservation orders: Courts are divided as to the standard for issuance of preservation orders. One line of cases holds that preservation orders are, in effect, case-management orders and are governed by Rule 16(b).[28] A few cases have handled preservation orders as injunctions.[29]

Spoliation and Sanctions

The flip side of data preservation is, of course, spoliation. Spoliation is "the destruction or material alteration of evidence or the failure to preserve property for another's use as evidence in pending or reasonably foreseeable litigation."[30] The authority to impose sanctions for spoliation arises under the Federal Rules of Civil Procedure and the court's inherent powers.[31] Determining whether

---

27. A court may be asked to issue an ex parte preservation order, but such orders should rarely be entered. The court is unlikely to have sufficient information about the responding party's computer system to be able to strike the correct balance between preservation and continued operation.

28. *See, e.g., Treppel*, 2006 WL 278170, *7; Capricorn Power Co. v. Siemens Westinghouse Power Corp., 220 F.R.D. 429, 433–34 (W.D. Pa. 2004); *Pueblo of Laguna*, 60 Fed. Cl. at 138 n.8.

29. *See In re* African-American Slave Descendants' Litig., 2003 U.S. Dist. LEXIS 12016, *7–8 (N.D. Ill. July 15, 2003).

30. Silvestri v. General Motors Corp., 271 F.3d 583, 590 (4th Cir. 2001).

31. Zubulake v. UBS Warburg, Inc. (*Zubulake IV*), 220 F.R.D. 212, 216 (S.D.N.Y. 2003).

sanctions are warranted for spoliation of ESI is challenging because it is easier to intentionally or inadvertently delete or modify ESI and it is more difficult for parties to craft preservation policies that ensure that the appropriate data are preserved.

The degree of scienter necessary to impose sanctions for spoliation is unsettled among the courts. For example, the Eighth Circuit Court of Appeals has held that an adverse inference instruction for destruction of evidence is available only when the destruction was intentional.[32] A New Jersey district court, in contrast, has affirmed the imposition of sanctions against the defendants, including an adverse inference instruction, without any finding of bad faith.[33] Similarly, the Second Circuit Court of Appeals has stated in dicta that ordinary negligence, as the result of which a party breaches a preservation obligation, is sanctionable.[34] In general, however, case law supports the notion that extreme sanctions are available only in extreme circumstances. Once a finding of spoliation has been made, courts will address whether the specific act of spoliation in question justifies an extreme sanction, such as an adverse inference jury instruction, issue preclusion, or judgment/ dismissal, rather than a less severe sanction, such as additional discovery with shifting of costs and a monetary sanction.[35]

Considering spoliation of ESI and sanctions:

Degree of scienter

Extent of prejudice

Relationship to records-management policy

Rule 37(f)

An issue that is likely to arise is whether spoliation sanctions should be imposed when evidence is destroyed in compliance with an established records-management policy. This, in turn, may lead to collateral discovery about whether such sanctions are warranted. One common function of computer systems is to delete certain information on an ongoing, prescheduled basis to prevent overloading the system (e.g., overwriting deleted digital informa-

---

32. Stevenson v. Union Pac. R.R. Co., 354 F.3d 739 (8th Cir. 2004); Morris v. Union Pac. R.R., 373 F.3d 896 (8th Cir. 2004).

33. Mosaid Techs. Inc. v. Samsung Electronics Co., 348 F. Supp. 2d 332 (D.N.J. 2004).

34. Residential Funding Corp. v. DeGeorge Fin. Corp., 306 F.3d 99, 108 (2d Cir. 2002).

35. See the Advisory Committee Note to the 1970 amendment to Rule 37 as it then existed (discussing *Societe Internationale v. Rogers*, 357 U.S. 197 (1958), and concluding that under Rule 37 "willfulness was relevant only to the selection of sanctions, if any, to be imposed").

tion, recycling backup tapes, and purging e-mails). Rule 37(f), ef-fective December 1, 2006, acknowledges such record-management policies, stating that *"absent exceptional circumstances,* a court may not impose sanctions under these rules on a party for failing to pro-vide electronically stored information lost as a result of the routine, *good-faith* operation of an electronic information system" (empha-sis added). Good faith may require, among other things, a party to modify or suspend certain features of the electronic information system to prevent the loss of information subject to preservation, and it may preclude a party from exploiting the routine operation of the system to thwart the party's discovery obligations. The lead-in phrase of the rule, "absent exceptional circumstances," provides the court with additional flexibility for dealing with rare, complex situations by allowing for sanctions in extraordinary circumstanc-es even if evidence was destroyed as a result of routine, good-faith operation of the system.

Conclusion

Discovery of ESI presents unique issues regarding the scope of dis-covery, the allocation of costs, the form of production, the waiver of privilege and work-product protection, and the preservation of data and spoliation. To effectively manage these issues, judges must understand the relevant technology at a level that allows ef-fective communication with attorneys, parties, and experts. The information in this guide is a start, and additional resources can be found on the Center's intranet site.

More specifically, judges must require attorneys to take seri-ously their obligation to meet and confer under Rule 26(f) and to submit a meaningful discovery plan that addresses ESI issues, and judges must ensure that adequate disclosures are made pursuant to Rule 26(a)(1). Judges must also encourage parties to narrowly target requests for ESI and to make these as early as possible in the litigation. Judges must evaluate whether the costs of comply-ing with the requests are proportional to their benefit. To this end, judges may need to encourage or order tiered discovery and sam-pling to determine the relevance, need, and cost of more expan-sive discovery, and may shift costs from the producing party to the requesting party, particularly when information that is not reasonably accessible must be produced. Judges need to help ensure that ESI is produced in a usable form, and, to facilitate efficient and cost-effective discovery, judges may need to clarify the procedures to be followed if privileged or protected information is inadvertently disclosed. They should help parties establish effective data-preservation policies, balancing the need to preserve relevant evidence and the need to continue routine computer operations critical to a party's activities, and enter preservation orders as appropriate.

In complex cases, these responsibilities are not easy undertakings. Thus, it may be appropriate for the judge to require parties to provide the judge with expert briefings on the relevant technological issues, and in some instances to seek the assistance of a special master or neutral expert. For example, the court may appoint a neutral expert to help develop a discovery plan and supervise technical aspects of discovery, review documents claimed to be privileged or protected, or participate in an on-site inspection.[36]

In the end, judges must actively manage electronic discovery—raising points for consideration by the parties—rather than awaiting the parties' identification and argument of the matters. Such active management can help ensure the expeditious and fair conduct of discovery involving ESI.

---

36. *See MCL 4th*, *supra* note 5, § 11.446, and *The Sedona Principles*, *supra* note 2, Comment 10.c.

Glossary

Note: Most entries in this glossary were derived, with permission, from a glossary prepared by the Sedona Conference. That extensive glossary, often with fuller definitions than presented here, is updated periodically and is available for download at www.thesedonaconference.org.

active data (active records): Information located in a computer system's memory or in storage media attached to the system (e.g., disk drives) that is readily available to the user, to the operating system, and to application software. (See *storage medium*.)

archival data: Information that is intentionally maintained in long-term storage for business, legal, regulatory, or similar purposes, but not immediately accessible to a computer system's user. May be stored on removable media, such as CDs, tapes, or removable disk drives, or may be maintained on system disk drives. Typically stored in an organized way to help identify, access, or retrieve individual records or files.

backup data (disaster recovery data): An exact copy of data that serves as a source for recovery in the event of a system problem or disaster. Generally stored separately from active data on, for example, tapes or removable disk drives, and often without indexes or other information and, as a result, in a form that makes it difficult to identify, access, or retrieve individual records or files.

backup tape recycling: A process in which backup data tapes are overwritten with new backup data, usually on a fixed schedule determined jointly by records-management, legal, and information technology (IT) sources.

computer forensics: The scientific examination and analysis of computerized data primarily for use as evidence. May include the secure collection of computer data; the examination of suspect data to determine details, such as origin and content; and the presentation of computer-based information to courts. May involve re-creating deleted, damaged, or missing files from disk drives; validating dates and authors/editors of documents; and certifying key elements of electronically stored information.

data (electronic): Information stored on a computer, including numbers, text, and images. Computer programs (e.g., word processing software, spreadsheet software, presentation software) are used to process, edit, or present data.

de-duplication: A process that searches for and deletes duplicate information. (See the glossary maintained by the Sedona Conference for a description of different types of de-duplication: www.thesedonaconference.org.)

deleted data: Data that once existed on a computer as active data, but have been marked as deleted by computer programs or user activity. Deleted data may remain on the storage media in whole or in part until they are overwritten or "wiped." Even after the data have been wiped, directory entries, pointers, or other information relating to the deleted data may remain on the computer.

deletion: A process in which data are marked as deleted by computer programs or user activity and made inaccessible except through the use of special data-recovery tools. Deletion makes data inaccessible with normal application programs, but commonly leaves the data itself on the storage medium. There are different degrees of deletion. "Soft deletions" are data marked as deleted in the computer operating system (and not generally available to the end-user after such marking), but not yet physically removed from or overwritten on the storage medium. Soft-deleted data can often be restored in their entirety. This can be contrasted with "wiping," a process that overwrites the deleted data with random digital characters, rendering it extremely difficult to recover, and "degaussing," which rearranges the magnetic patterns on the medium, rendering it impossible to recover with all but the most sophisticated computer forensics tools.

electronic discovery: The process of collecting, preparing, reviewing, and producing electronic documents in a variety of criminal and civil actions and proceedings.

embedded data: Data that include commands that control or manipulate data, such as computational formulas in spreadsheets or formatting commands in a word processing document. Not visible when a document is printed or saved as an image format. (See *metadata*.)

ESI: Electronically stored information.

file format: The internal organization, characteristics, and structure of a file that determine the software programs with which it can optimally be used, viewed, or manipulated. The simplest file format is ASCII (American Standard Code for Information Interchange; pronounced "ASK-ee"), a nonproprietary text format. Documents in ASCII consist of only text with no formatting or graphics and can be read by most computer systems using nonproprietary applications. Specific applications may define unique (and proprietary) formats for their data (e.g., WordPerfect document file format). Files with unique formats may only be viewed or printed by using their originating application or an application designed to work with compatible formats. These formats are also called the "native" format. Computer systems commonly identify files by a naming convention that denotes the native format (and therefore the probable originating application). For example, a WordPerfect document could be named document.wpd, where .wpd denotes a WordPerfect file format. Other common formats are .xls for Microsoft Excel spreadsheet files, .txt for ASCII text files, .ppt for Microsoft PowerPoint files, .jpg for photographs or other images, and .pdf for Adobe Acrobat documents.

form of production: The manner in which requested documents are produced. Used to refer to both file format and the media on which the documents are produced (paper vs. electronic).

hash value: A unique numerical identifier that can be assigned to a file, a group of files, or a portion of a file, based on a standard mathematical algorithm applied to the characteristics of the data set. The most commonly used algorithms, known as MD5 and SHA, will generate numerical values so distinctive that the chance that any two data sets will have the same hash value, no matter how similar they appear, is less than one in one billion. "Hashing" is used to guarantee the authenticity of an original data set and can be used as a digital equivalent of the Bates stamp used in paper document production.

image (verb): To image a hard drive is to make an identical copy of the hard drive at the lowest level of data storage. The image will include deleted data, residual data, and data found in hidden portions of the hard drive. Also known as creating a "bitstream image" or "mirror image," or "mirroring" the drive. It is different than the process of making a "logical copy" or "ghosting" a hard drive, which normally copies only the active data found on the hard drive, and not the deleted data, residual data, and data found in hidden portions of the hard drive.

legacy data: Information in which an organization may have invested significant resources to develop and which retains importance, but which was created and is stored with software and/or hardware that has become obsolete or replaced ("legacy systems"). May be costly to restore or reconstruct.

metadata: Information about a particular data set or document which describes how, when, and by whom the data set or document was collected, created, accessed, or modified; its size; and how it is formatted. Some metadata, such as file dates and sizes, can easily be seen by users; other metadata can be hidden from users but are still available to the operating system or the program used to process the data set or document. (See *embedded data* and *systems data*.)

nearline data storage: Storage in a system that is not physically part of the computer system or local network in daily use, but can be accessed through the network. Nearline data may be stored in a library of CDs, which can be automatically located and mounted for reading, or stored at a remote location accessible through an Internet connection. There is usually a small time lag between the request for data stored in nearline media and the data's availability to an application or end-user. Making nearline data available is an automated process (as opposed to "offline" data, which can only be made available by a person physically retrieving the data).

offline storage: The storage of electronic records, often for long-term archival purposes, on removable media (e.g., CDs, removable disk drives) or magnetic tape that is not connected to a computer or network. Accessibility to off-line media usually requires manual intervention and is much slower than online or nearline storage, depending on how and where the media are stored.

PDF (portable document format): A file format developed by Adobe Systems Incorporated. Documents, once converted to this format, are readable outside of the application that created them. A PDF file captures document formatting information (e.g., margins, spacing, fonts) from the original application (e.g., WordPerfect) in such a way that the document can be viewed and printed as intended in the original application by the Adobe Reader program, which is available for most computer operating systems. Other programs (notably Adobe Acrobat) are required to edit or otherwise manipulate a PDF file.

records management: The activities involved in handling information, generally for organizations that are large data producers. Records management includes maintaining, organizing, preserving, and destroying information, regardless of its form or the medium on which it is stored.

residual data (ambient data): Data that are not active on a computer system and that are not visible without use of "undelete" or other special data-recovery techniques. May contain copies of deleted files, Internet files, and file fragments.

restore: To transfer data from a backup or archival storage system (e.g., tapes) to an online system. Restoration of archival data may require not only data restoration but also replication of the original hardware and software operating environment.

sampling: A process of selecting and searching a small part of a larger data source to test for the existence or frequency of relevant information, to assess whether the source contains privileged or protected information, and to assess the costs and burdens of identifying and producing requested information.

search engine: A program that enables a search for keywords or phrases, such as on webpages throughout the World Wide Web. (See the glossary maintained by the Sedona Conference for a description of different types of searches: www.thesedonaconference.org.)

storage medium: The physical device containing ESI, including computer memory, disk drives (including removable disk drives), magneto-optical media, CDs, DVDs, memory sticks, and tapes.

systems data: Information about a computer system that includes, for example, when people logged on and off a computer or network, the applications and passwords they used, and what websites they visited.

About the Federal Judicial Center

The Federal Judicial Center is the research and education agency of the federal judicial system. It was established by Congress in 1967 (28 U.S.C. §§ 620–629), on the recommendation of the Judicial Conference of the United States.

By statute, the Chief Justice of the United States chairs the Center's Board, which also includes the director of the Administrative Office of the U.S. Courts and seven judges elected by the Judicial Conference.

The organization of the Center reflects its primary statutory mandates. The Education Division plans and produces education and training programs for judges and court staff, including satellite broadcasts, video programs, publications, curriculum packages for in-court training, and Web-based programs and resources. The Research Division examines and evaluates current and alternative federal court practices and policies. This research assists Judicial Conference committees, who request most Center research, in developing policy recommendations. The Center's research also contributes substantially to its educational programs. The two divisions work closely with two units of the Director's Office—the Systems Innovations & Development Office and Communications Policy & Design Office—in using print, broadcast, and online media to deliver education and training and to disseminate the results of Center research. The Federal Judicial History Office helps courts and others study and preserve federal judicial history. The International Judicial Relations Office provides information to judicial and legal officials from foreign countries and assesses how to inform federal judicial personnel of developments in international law and other court systems that may affect their work.